MAKING A WILL
a n d
CREATING
ESTATE PLANS

THE NO NONSENSE LIBRARY

NO NONSENSE CAREER GUIDES

Managing Time
No Nonsense Management
How to Choose a Career
How to Re-enter the Workforce
How to Write a Resume
No Nonsense Interviewing

NO NONSENSE FINANCIAL GUIDES

How to Use Credit and Credit Cards
Investing in Mutual Funds
Investing in the Stock Market
Investing in Tax Free Bonds
Understanding Money Market Funds
Understanding IRA's
Understanding Treasury Bills and Other U.S. Government Securities
Understanding Common Stocks
Understanding Stock Options and Futures Markets
Understanding Social Security
Understanding Insurance
How to Plan and Invest for Your Retirement
Making a Will and Creating Estate Plans

NO NONSENSE REAL ESTATE GUIDES

Understanding Condominiums and Co-ops
How to Buy a Home
Understanding Mortgages and Home Equity Loans

NO NONSENSE SUCCESS GUIDES

NO NONSENSE HEALTH GUIDES

NO NONSENSE COOKING GUIDES

NO NONSENSE PARENTING GUIDES

NO NONSENSE CAR GUIDES

NO NONSENSE FINANCIAL GUIDE ™

MAKING A WILL

and

CREATING ESTATE PLANS

Harvey J. Platt

The author would like to acknowledge Andrew L. Platt and James Preston for their assistance in the research for this project.

Cover design by Nancy Sabato
Interior design by Richard Oriolo

ISBN: 0-681-41399-9
Printed in the United States of America
First Edition

0 9 8 7 6 5 4 3 2 1

CONTENTS

MAKING A WILL

a n d

CREATING ESTATE PLANS

CHAPTER I

UNDERSTANDING ESTATE PLANNING AND WILLS

WHAT IS ESTATE PLANNING?

No individual can predict their own death. In fact, death is a subject that many people do not want to discuss or even think about, and this can lead to problems when they have not prepared for the inevitable. Estate planning is the process that prepares individuals and their families for the transfer of their property and possessions (the "estate") at death. Estate planning is required in order to oversee the orderly distribution of that property and, in many instances, to lessen the enormous impact of federal estate taxes and state inheritance taxes.

Fear of death can have a very large psychological

effect on people; even worse is the fear of death without proper estate planning. Estate planning will relieve an individual's anxiety that their family and friends will not receive their property and possessions. A good estate plan will accomplish the distribution of their property according to their wishes and intentions, while providing their beneficiaries with the maximum shelter against estate taxation.

The basic instrument of the estate-planning process is the will. A will is probably the most personal legal expression of a person's feelings toward family, relatives, and friends that each and every individual will need to complete. If a person fails to prepare a will, on death state intestacy laws will provide for the distribution of their property. This could lead to disastrous effects, since the state's order of distribution of the decedent's property may be totally against the wishes of that person.

Additionally, the failure to execute a will and properly plan for the estate's distribution could increase the estate taxes payable to the federal and state estate-taxing authorities. Presently, the Federal Estate Tax is the most expensive tax in the country. (Its top rate of 55 percent will remain until after December 31, 1992; the top rate is scheduled to drop to 50 percent.) If a person fails to properly plan for death, federal and state governments can take a large portion of the estate, possibly wiping out any inheritance or the passing on of any property.

There are some basic questions that have to be asked before preparing a will and an estate plan. These questions are necessary for an understanding of the nature of the property and the possessions involved, and the desires for their distribution. The most significant question is, What do I own? These are the assets of your estate. You must be sure to know whether you really own these items or if they are jointly held with a spouse, or another person.

If there are any assets that heirs do not know about, such as a secret bank account, it is imperative to tell somebody, either a relative or a lawyer, of its existence and location. Other areas of special concern that must be examined as well are: any business that you may own or have an interest in, employment compensation agreements and any retirement or other deferred-benefit plans.

The next question that must be asked is, Who should inherit these items? And decisions have to be made whether or not children or grandchildren are old enough to handle assets they would inherit. As well, it is necessary to consider the possible re-marriage of a spouse. Although always necessary, estate planning is often crucial for individuals who are in second or subsequent marriages and have children from a prior marriage.

Another question that might be asked is whether or not you intend to leave any gifts to close friends, or to charities. If a person plans to make bequests of this type and fails to properly execute a will, state intestacy laws will not provide for them and these wishes will not be carried out.

The last question to ask is, Who will carry out my wishes? An executor, or personal representative, is named in a will and has the legal duty of administering the estate. After death, this individual or institution starts the probate or administration process by

1. opening the estate by offering the will to the court;

2. collecting the decedent's assets;
3. paying any family allowance and setting aside the homestead and personal property exemptions;
4. paying creditors' claims and tax bills;
5. distributing the assets of the estate with the Court entering a decree of distribution.

Remember: It is important to note that inheritance is not a natural right. There is nothing in our laws that require a parent to leave anything to a child—in most jurisdictions. However, in most instances, our laws do protect spouses.

An understanding of the legal process of death is one of the most difficult areas of law for individuals to comprehend. Hopefully, this book will enable you to understand what estate planning is, discover what choices you will have in determining the best plan for your estate, and develop a general comprehension of the legal aspects of wills, estates, and trust laws.

CHAPTER II

INTESTACY: WHO CAN COLLECT WHEN THERE IS NO WILL

All states have statutes of descent that govern the distribution of the property of a person who dies without a will, or who had not made a complete testamentory disposition of the testate estate. A person so dying is deemed to have died intestate. It is very important to know whether a will exists, because the order of distribution under the intestacy laws may contradict the wishes that the decedent may have had for the distribution of their property.

In intestacy, real and personal property passes as a tenancy in common because no specific right of survivorship is established before death, such as joint tenancy.

Each state has specific rules regarding intestacy,

but there are common themes that run throughout all state laws. For instance, under the ancient common law of England which formed the original laws of most states, a spouse was not an heir, and the decedent's property passed by intestacy to descendants, such as children. Today, most jurisdictions protect the surviving spouse by permitting the survivor to take an intestate or "elective" share of the decedent's estate.

And in most jurisdictions, after the spouse's share, children will inherit the remainder of the decedent's property to the exclusion of everyone else. Also, in most jurisdictions, parents do not inherit when the decedent is survived by descendants.

If the decedent is not survived by a spouse, descendants, or parents, intestate property will usually pass to brothers, sisters, or their descendants, or other more distant relatives.

If there are no heirs, the property of the decedent will escheat (pass to the state) in all jurisdictions.

Another important aspect of intestacy law is that in some jurisdictions if a spouse is abandoned and such abandonment continued until the time of death, rights to such abandoned spouse's estate may be lost even if the parties were still married. New York is one such state that adheres to this rule.

Generally, a person will be entitled to inherit the property of an intestate decedent only if that person survives the decedent. Problems in determining the order of death have developed as the result of common disasters, such as accidents in trains, airplanes, and cars. Therefore, the Uniform Simultaneous Death Act was enacted, which provides that where there is no sufficient evidence of the order of deaths, the beneficiary is deemed to have predeceased the benefactor.

Each state has a different standard to determine the order of deaths. Under the Uniform Probate Code an individual needs to survive by 120 hours to be a testate heir.

Intestacy laws specify exactly which classes of surviving relatives will receive the assets of an intestate estate. Where all of the living descendants are members of the same generation, most American statutes provide for a per capita distribution of the assets. In a per capita jurisdiction the estate is equally divided based on the number of takers. Under a per stirpes distribution, or a "by the roots" distribution, remote descendants take what their ancestor would have taken. The courts have defined the term "per stirpes" to mean that assets are divided at the generational level. So that a distribution of property is, per stirpes, when it is made to a person who receives the same as a descendant, the share which his or her ancestor would have taken had he or she been alive at the time. For example, a disposition to the testator's cousin's who are named in the will "in equal shares, per stirpes", would not terminate as to a named cousin who predeceases the testator. This is so because the will clearly indicates the intention of the testator that the heirs of a deceased cousin would receive the gift in place of the named cousin.

Today, in many states, a child conceived during the father's lifetime but born after his death is considered the decedent/father's child for inheritance purposes. These children are called "posthumous children."

In all states that have enacted statutes governing inheritance rights of adopted children, an adopted child has the same rights as a natural child. The law in some states is that once adopted, you are completely severed from your natural parents and cannot inherit from the prior family; the natural parents relinquish all rights to their natural child's estate, as well.

However, where an adoptee is adopted within the family, he or she may still inherit from certain members of the natural family. Only a few adoption or inheritance statutes draw a distinction between adoption of a minor and an adult.

Occasionally, the adoption of an adult may be useful in preventing a will contest. If a testator adopts a child, the testator's collateral relatives may not contest the proceeding since the adoptee can now inherit through intestacy and thereby exclude their prospective intestacy rights.

Usually the only persons who have standing to challenge the validity of a will are those who would inherit an intestate decedent's property if the will was denied validity by the court and not declared the "Last Will and Testament" of the decedent. However, some states have challenged this concept. (In New York, for example, an adult male cannot adopt a male lover, although the adoption of a friend to whom you wish to leave property is often done to avoid a legal contest. But in the case of homosexual lovers, this practice has been limited by the courts on the grounds of its being against the public policy of the state.)

A stepchild can inherit under the laws of some states if the intestate has no close blood relatives. Under California law, a stepchild or a foster child is permitted to take a child's share: (1) if the relationship between parent and child began during the person's minority and continued throughout the parties' joint lifetimes; (2) if it is established by clear and convincing evidence that the foster parent or stepparent would have adopted that person but for a legal barrier.

In most states today, a child born out of wedlock inherits from his or her natural mother and the mother's kin, and they in turn can inherit from and through the child. For these so-called illegitimate children, the rules of inheritance from their father vary from state to state.

Generally, most states hold that an illegitimate child can inherit from their father: (1) if there is a court order covering affiliation (such as a paternity suit); (2) if the father signs and registers with a court that the child is his heir, (3) if there is clear and convincing evidence that the father acknowledges the child as a family member.

Only one of the above criteria must be met for a child to inherit. However in New York State, a parent who abandons a child will not inherit from the estate of that child.

Generally, there are three types of circumstances where transfers to minors require examination. The first deals with a person who dies intestate. In this instance a guardian must be appointed to receive and manage any of the intestate decedent's property that passes to a minor heir. In addition, if there are no surviving parents a guardian needs to be appointed for the child's custody until he or she attains the age of majority.

States that follow the Uniform Probate Code restrict the term "guardian" to mean "guardian of the person." The Code renames the guardian of a minor's property "conservator of a protected person" who, under the statute, is given powers and duties comparable to those of a Trustee. Court appointment and supervision is still required, but legal obligations and requirements are more flexible than that of a guardian and only requires an annual accounting.

The second type of transfer to a minor is under a gift transaction. Since a minor usually cannot hold title to property the gift of such property is made to a Custodian. A "custodian" is the person who is given the property to hold for the benefit of the minor under the state's Uniform Transfers and Gifts to Minors Act. Custodians are given statutory powers like a Trustee's and, therefore, can spend income or principal for the support of the minor.

It is important to understand the difference between these two legal arrangements. In a custodial situation the custodian is not under the supervision of the court, as is a guardian or a conservator, and usually no annual or final accounting is necessary until the minor reaches the age of majority, which is usually eighteen.

The third type of transfer to a minor takes place in the form of a trust, and it is the most flexible property arrangement of the three. In a trust, property is held for the benefit of the minor. If the minor dies this property usually passes to the minor's heirs, and if there are none, to the siblings of the minor.

CHAPTER III

WHAT IS A WILL AND WHY HAVE ONE?

Generally, a will is a set of words that describes how an individual's estate will be disposed of or distributed among family and friends. As it is the key instrument for the transfer of property at death, the best way to think of it is as the written instructions legally formalized under the legal rules of the testator's state, that will guide the disposition of the estate. In order for this document to be a valid set of instructions, a will has to be properly executed.

The first requirement is that the testator (the individual who creates the will) needs to be of "sound mind." Mental capacity is required for the protection of society and for the protection of the decedent's family as well as the decedent.

The general test of adequate mental capacity is that the testator must know the following: (1) the nature and extent of their property; (2) the persons who are the natural objects of their bounty (those who would inherit the decedent's assets if there was no will); (3) the disposition which they are making; (4) how these elements relate so as to form an orderly plan for the disposition of the property being passed on. If the testator lacks any capacity to understand these questions then the testator lacks the proper mental capacity to execute a will.

After a will has been written, it needs to be signed by the testator and, in most states, by two witnesses, following a formal attestation (signing) procedure. Most states have strict requirements for due execution of wills. For a will to be valid and admissible by the courts, the testator must meet the formal requirements of due execution imposed by the statutes of each state.

The Uniform Probate Code requires that every will shall be in writing and signed by the testator or signed in the testator's name by some other person in the testator's presence. And it requires that the will be signed by at least two persons, each of whom has witnessed either the signing itself or the testator's acknowledgment of the signature. The one exception to this rule is holographic wills, which are documents handwritten by the testator and which will be discussed later on.

Some states have different requirements as to what constitutes a valid signature; for example, in New York an initial is a valid signature. In all jurisdictions a testator must sign the will at the end of the document. However, if there are additional provisions or writings after the signature, the will is not invalidated as to the provisions before the signature, only what is contained after is invalid.

Like the testator, the witnesses must be competent. This generally means that at the time the will is executed the witnesses must be mature enough and of sufficient mental capacity to understand and appreciate the nature of the act they are witnessing and be able to testify in court should it be necessary.

A person who receives any benefit under the will should not be a witness to the instrument. This is a common mistake in will executions. At English common law, if a witness was also a beneficiary of a will, they were deemed not a competent witness and the will was denied validity by the Courts. Today however most jurisdictions have interested witness statutes, which provide that if an attesting witness is also a beneficiary, the gift to the person is void but the witness is a competent witness and the will may be declared valid. Such forfeiting witness, may, however, receive such gift under the laws of intestacy.

Each state may vary as to the requirements of being disinterested. In the states of New York and Massachusetts any one interested in the will can be a witness and testify but any disposition made for this person is void unless two other attesting witnesses are disinterested at the time of execution. Under the Uniform Probate Code a competent interested person can still receive their share as set forth in the will and the document in considered valid. The problem with taking the share away from an interested witness is the retribution factor. The witness may then attempt to have the will invalidated and as a witness may have the power to do so.

The appropriate formality of execution is to have all persons in the same room and all sign the document, using the same pen, and have the testator sign or initial each page. Also, after a will has been executed it should never be taken apart once it has been stapled together.

In the execution of a will the state laws of the decedent's domicile at death determine the validity of the will insofar as it disposes of personal property. But the laws of each state where real property owned by the decedent is located determines the validity of the disposition of that real property. Hence, a will should be executed so that it will be valid in all jurisdictions involved.

The great majority of states have adopted a self-proving will procedure. After executing the will, the testator and the witnesses execute, in the presence of a notary public, an affidavit reciting that all of the requisites for due execution have been complied with. If this is done certain formalities required by the Courts in the proving of a will may be dispensed with.

Once a will has been executed, it is important to safeguard it. Most states that had statutes restricting the probate of lost wills have repealed them. However, even if a will is lost, or destroyed without the consent of the testator, in many states this does not prevent its probate, provided its contents are proved. But a will should be safeguarded—usually by the lawyer who prepared it. A will placed in a safe deposit box may not be conveniently available to the heirs, since safe deposit boxes may under local law be sealed for a period of time after the death of the box holder.

WHAT TO INCLUDE

The most important question that needs to be asked when making a will is what should be included. Although each will is different, there are certain fundamental aspects and key provisions included in all wills.

Each will should arrange for the disposition of all assets of the person's estate and it should include any special requests, such as burial directions. This will avoid any problems with the beneficiaries of the estate and stop any potential disposition of property through intestacy.

As well, each will should state who are the individuals who should inherit the estate. This is very important, as it will help avoid any problems among intended beneficiaries, as well as those with family and friends who think they are going to be beneficiaries and, in fact, are not.

The will also needs to name the executors, or personal representatives, of the estate. An executor is a person (or institution) appointed in the will to carry out the estate plan, which puts this person in a fiduciary relationship with the estate. This is a legal duty that makes the appointee responsible for carrying out all of the required procedures in the administration of the estate. Generally, each spouse will elect the other to be the legal representative of the other's estate, and one or more of their children, if they have any, to be the successors. Choosing the estate's representative and the successor may be the most important decision made when making a will.

A will also needs to appoint guardians if there are any minors that survive after the parents are no longer there. A guardian is responsible for both person and property. This can be the same person or two different people. Choosing a guardian is probably more important that appointing an executor because it involves making decisions concerning the children of the deceased parents. Guardians of the property inherited by minor children need to be appointed in the state where the property is located.

A will should also dispose of a testator's personal property. This can be done by making certain specific bequests, or it can be achieved through a residuary clause. A residuary clause disposes of all the remaining estate after specific bequests are made and all expenses are paid, including medical bills, taxes, and debts. Generally, this is called the "residue." So if a will contains a residuary clause it has to name a residuary beneficiary, as well.

A will can provide gifts to specific beneficiaries. Under traditional rules of testate law there are three separate and distinct terms for giving personal and real property under a will. There is a devise, which directs the disposition of real property, and the person named to receive the real property is called the devisee. Then there is the legacy, which is a clause that directs the disposition of money. And third, there is a bequest, a clause directing the disposition of personal property other than money.

WRITING THE WILL

Perceiving a public demand for a legally valid will that can be written on a printed form that is easily available, several states have authorized simple "statutory wills." In a statutory will spaces are provided where the testator simply writes in the names of the beneficiaries. But these instruments have been highly debated in the legal profession because they can create a great deal of problems. Individuals should not try to write their own wills, as they may do more harm than good. Trying to cut corners in the making of a will could create great problems for the testator's estate.

HOLOGRAPHIC WILLS

A holographic will is one written entirely in the testator's hand and signed by the testator. Generally, in states that recognize holographic wills attesting witnesses are not required. The rationale is that it is difficult to forge a person's handwriting.

About half of the states permit holographic wills. In those states, a holographic will supersedes a prior formally executed will. Under the Uniform Probate Code, a holographic will is valid, whether or not it has been witnessed, if the signature and the material provisions are in the handwriting of the testator. If the printed material were eliminated, the handwritten portion must evidence the testator's intentions, and the key dispositive provision must be in the testator's handwriting. (In a holographic will the key dispositive positions must be in the testator's handwriting.) Check your state's Attorneys office to verify the validity of holographic wills.

UPDATING A WILL

A will is a document that periodically needs to be reviewed, updated, and revised to reflect the changes that occur during our lifetimes. Updating a will should be done at the same time as the update of an estate plan. It is important to update these not only to maximize the benefits of any changes in the tax laws, but also to insure that the will and estate plan reflect one's true wishes for all family members and friends. A will is a transitory piece of paper that can be updated at any time. Once properly executed, the latest will is the one that counts. Wills and estate plans should be reviewed every few years.

A will may be updated by preparing an entirely new will or by adding a codicil. A codicil is a written document that changes existing provisions of one's will without redoing the entire document. In times past codicils were very common as it was very costly to change the whole will. As the word processor has facilitated the ability to update documents, codicils are less recommended. If the execution of a wholly new document will cause the testator's estate to lose the benefits of an existing tax law, a codicil should be executed to protect against such loss.

Under the Uniform Probate Code revocation of a will is completed by a subsequent will, which revokes the prior will; or by a physical act where the will is burned, torn, canceled, obliterated, or destroyed, with the intent of, and for the purpose of, revoking it by the testator or by another person in the testator's presence and at direction of the testator.

As well, a will can be revoked by operation of law. If the testator gets married or divorced after executing a will, this change in status may revoke, by operation of law, all or part of the will. Generally, each state has laws covering the effect of a change in status on an existing will.

As stated previously, a will may be revoked or changed by a later will or codicil. In these instances, language which expressly revokes the prior will should be included. Alternatively, a later will may revoke a prior will if there are inconsistent provisions in the later will that implicitly revoke the earlier will.

It is important to note that if an updated will is lost, the prior will may be the executed document offered to the courts. However, some states have laws concerning the valid declaration of lost wills. Generally, in the absence of a statute, a will that is lost, or destroyed without the consent of the testator, or destroyed with the consent of the testator but not in compliance with the revocation statute can be admitted into probate if its contents are proved.

Under common law the rule was that when a will was revoked, a codicil to it also failed. But when a codicil was destroyed the will's integrity remained and was therefore valid.

Another important point to note is that a will should never be executed in duplicate. There should never be more than one original copy in existence. Duplicate wills can create problems with destruction and amendments. In one jurisdiction the law holds that there is a presumption that where there is only a duplicate and the original is lost, the will is presumed destroyed, even though this may not have been the decedent's belief at the time of death.

REVOCATION OF WILLS

Writing on a will "this will is null and void" may not be a valid revocation of a will. In one jurisdiction a person

attempted revocation by writing on the pages upon
which the will was written, but the law was such that
a revocation of a will by cancellation was not accomplished unless the words of the document are muti-
lated or otherwise impaired. Wills may need to be
destroyed by a physical act.

It is important to note that there may be no
mutilation of a will when the word "Canceled" is
written in the margin of the document. There may
need to be a writing on the words in the will. But in a
state that recognizes holographic wills, writing "I
revoke" is enough to revoke a will. However, writing
"Destroy" is not enough to revoke the will.

In New York State there is no partial revocation
by a physical act, and total revocation needs two
witnesses. However, some states do recognize partial
revocation by a physical act. Although the Uniform
Probate Code and the statutes of a number of states
authorize partial revocation by physical act, in several
states a will cannot be revoked in part by an act of
revocation; it can be revoked in part only by a subsequent instrument. Remember, the signature is the
most vulnerable part of a will!!

There is a doctrine, which certain jurisdictions
recognize, acknowledging that people sometimes revoke a will by mistake. This doctrine is called the
Dependent Relative Revocation and Revival. Under
this doctrine a court may disregard a revocation if the
court finds that the act of revocation was premised on
a mistake of law or fact, and that it would not have
occurred but for the testator's mistaken belief that
another disposition of property was valid.

SPECIAL SITUATIONS

Some states still recognize mortmain statutes, which are derived from the feudal system. These statutes protect the testator from making deathbed gifts. Generally, they were enacted because there were fears of gifts of this nature to charities, and under these laws any such gifts made ninety days before death were void. These statutes were basically antireligious, as a religious leader generally had the chance to influence a dying person to give to the religious organization.

In New York State, if a marriage is ended by divorce, then all provisions to a spouse in a will are void. In some states the law is as if the former spouse predeceased the decedent, so as to protect the children and the estate plan. In other states, the transfer to the former spouse is just "null and void." But in a life insurance policy, the former spouse named as the beneficiary will be held as the beneficiary by contract law.

What happens if a person executes a will and subsequently marries? A large majority of states have statutes giving the spouse an intestate share, unless it appears from the will that the omission was intentional, or if the spouse is provided for in the will or by a will substitute, which is a transfer in lieu of a will provision. Examples of this are a trust or annuity created during the life of the testator for the benefit of the surviving spouse, whereby its income is payable for the life of the surviving spouse.

The Doctrine of Incorporation By Reference is a doctrine whereby pages that cannot be integrated because they were not present at the will's execution nevertheless may be given effect. This doctrine recognizes that a duly executed will may, by appropriate reference, incorporate into itself any extrinsic document or writing, even though the other document was not similarly executed.

However, the following requirements must be met: (1) the document must have been in existence at the time the will was executed; (2) the will must expressly refer to the document in the present tense; (3) the will must describe the document to be incorporated so clearly that there can be no mistake as to the identity of the document referred to; (4) the testator must have intended to incorporate the extrinsic document as part of the overall testimentary plan.

Under the Uniform Probate Code, any writing in existence when a will is executed may be incorporated by reference if the language of the will manifests this intent and describes the writing sufficiently to permit its identification. Note that this is not the law in the states of Texas, Louisiana and New York.

However, the testator may refer to a separate memorandum disposing of his or her personal property, and if such memorandum is attached to other pages of the will and was present at execution, such memorandum is entitled to probate under the doctrine of integration.

A contract to make a will or not to revoke a will are kinds of agreements people enter into pertaining to wills. In these instances, the law of contracts will apply. A will in violation of a valid contract made by the testator, while it may be probated, will be subject to contractual remedies, for example, the imposition of a constructive trust.

These contracts typically arise when a husband

and wife have executed joint and mutual wills. A number of states have enacted statutes requiring that any agreement relating to a will, including a contract not to revoke a will, be in writing and executed with certain formalities. The mere execution of reciprocal wills containing identical provisions does not constitute evidence that the will was made on a contractual basis.

A joint will is a will of two or more persons that is executed as a single testamentary instrument. In contrast to joint wills, reciprocal wills (sometimes called mutual, or mirror, wills), are separate wills of two or more persons which contain reciprocal provisions. A joint and mutual will is a single will made by two people, under which each person leaves their property according to the terms of the will. Mutuality must be specifically stated in order for it to be deemed a contract. A party who is clearly and unambiguously bound to the provisions of a joint and mutual will may not alter the testamentary plan after the death of the other participant in the joint plan.

The Uniform Probate Code holds that a contract to make a will or devise, or not to revoke a will or devise, or not to die intestate can be established by (1) provisions of a will stating material provisions of the contract; (2) an express reference in a will to a contract and extrinsic evidence proving the terms of the contract; (3) a writing signed by the testator evidencing the contract. The execution of a joint will or mutual wills does not create a presumption of a contract not to revoke the will or wills.

CHAPTER IV

PROBATE

THE PROCESS OF PROBATE

The purpose of the legal process of probate is to ensure that the transfer of the entire estate of an individual is complete and unobstructed. Remember, completion of this procedure also requires that property passing outside of the will (outside of probate) is also unobstructed as well. Estate planning can be looked at as more of a preventative process, beginning long before probate, as one of its main goals is to avoid any possible future contests to the distribution of the estate property, either by the courts or by other interested individuals.

There are numerous grounds on which a court,

individual, or other entity may contest a will. There
may be some uncertainty as to whether the will being
offered for the court's approval was the last properly
executed will of the decedent. Questions may be
raised regarding the competency of the testator or the
testator's compliance with the relevant formalities of
execution required by law. Ambiguities in the document itself may also give rise to disputes.

Accordingly, it is crucial that all steps are taken
by the estate planner early on to ensure a smooth
passage of estate property in the future either
through or outside of probate. There can be many
costly pitfalls if estate planning is done improperly.
Professional legal expertise is essential in the planning
stage.

The probate process itself can be time-consuming
and expensive. Probate begins when a prospective
will is brought before the court after the testator has
died. The probate court will determine whether or not
the proposed document is a valid will. If the will is
deemed valid then the document's assets will pass, to
the extent possible, as directed therein. If a will is not
deemed to be valid then the descendent's property will
pass through intestacy. Either way, however, the
estate is handled by the probate court. There is no
time limit in most states as to how long after the
decedent's death a will may be entered into probate.

The decedent's estate must be represented in
probate by an agent, which is the executor or personal
representative named in the will by the testator. In
the absence of a will the Court appoints an administrator to administer the affairs of the decedent, usually the closest relative to the decedent.

The responsibilities of the agent are broad. The

agent must essentially take over all management functions of the estate in accordance with any instructions the probate court may choose to issue. Further, the agent must complete or close out any unfinished business or other obligations of the decedent to the extent that is possible. Also, all estate debts, including taxes, contract obligations, and other payable accounts and expenses, must be settled.

Selecting a competent and responsible agent is very important. Remember, the agent must be qualified to handle all the management, administrative, and accounting duties necessary to properly complete the probate process. Therefore, having an agent with professional knowledge and experience in such matters will avoid costly and time-consuming mistakes.

THE EXPENSES OF PROBATE

There are many costs that arise during probate, which some will substitutes, such as an inter-vivos trust or life insurance policy, or survivorship bank accounts are not subject to. The persons employed in the administration of the estate have to be paid. This includes the agent, whose charges or commissions are usually fixed by statute, and any other professionals that may be involved in the probate process such as appraisers, accountants, and attorneys. Most lawyers will charge an hourly rate for their services in handling the administration of an estate. Others may charge a flat percentage of the gross estate. There will also be court-processing fees and other transaction costs that an estate is required to incur during the probate period. In some states, probate fees may be

determined by statute or by order of the court. The
extent of these costs will vary depending on the size
and complexity of the estate and the state in which it
is administered. The costs of the probate process can
be reduced by transferring assets during one's lifetime, therefore not directly owning them at the time
of death.

CHAPTER V

BENEFICIARIES AND LIMITS ON ESTATE DISTRIBUTIONS

A beneficiary is a person or entity that has been selected by the testator to receive all or a portion of the estate upon the testator's death. Generally, a beneficiary will be unaware of the right to share in the decedent's estate until the will has been admitted to probate. The testator has great freedom in selecting beneficiaries of choice. In general, beneficiaries may be family members, relatives, friends, charities, trusts, and other organizations. However, depending upon the state in which one lives, there are some restrictions controlling estate distributions. These will be discussed below.

Selecting the beneficiary of an estate is an extremely important aspect of the overall estate plan.

This selection process should be used to provide as much certainty as possible regarding the disposition of the estate while at the same time fulfilling all distribution wishes. Important considerations include the likelihood that the bequests and devises made will be given effect by the probate court, the subsequent federal estate tax consequences, the effects such bequests and devises will have upon those who survive, and any special needs of friends or dependents.

CONTINGENT BENEFICIARIES

There is no guarantee that a beneficiary will survive the testator. If a beneficiary dies before the testator, the bequest to that beneficiary is said to have "lapsed." Unless the testator has selected a "contingent" or alternate beneficiary, the lapsed portion of the estate will either pass through a residuary clause in the will, or through intestacy if there is no residuary clause. One other possibility is that the state in which one resides at the time of death may have an antilapse statute. Such a statute would prevent certain devises from lapsing. For example, in New York State bequests to predeceased issue or to brothers and sisters will not lapse. In such cases, if the issue or sibling predeceases the testator, the bequest will pass to their respective heirs.

WHO SURVIVES WHOM?

As in intestacy, there are situations where the testator and a prospective beneficiary may die at, or almost at, the same time. This usually occurs in a mutual accident or by coincidence. In general, most states will honor a bequest to a beneficiary who survives the testator even for any instant of time. However, as previously indicated, states that follow the Uniform Probate Code require the beneficiary to survive the testator by 120 hours. This means that if one is in a Uniform Probate Code state and a beneficiary dies two days after the decedent, the bequest to that person fails. It is as if that person died before the decedent, even though he or she did not.

THE RESIDUARY CLAUSE

The residuary clause is one that may be incorporated into the will, functioning as a blanket contingency should any bequest or contingent bequest fail. A bequest that fails, for whatever reason, would turn over into the residue of the estate. As previously mentioned, this residue also includes any assets not specifically accounted for in the will. Therefore it is important that the testator select a residuary beneficiary.

It is always a good idea to incorporate a residuary clause into the will even if one has selected contingent beneficiaries for all bequests. There is always the possibility that a contingent beneficiary will predecease the testator. Furthermore, even if all beneficiaries do survive the testator, there may still be estate assets remaining that were not disposed of, and therefore could be subject to intestacy, or may "escheat" in the absence of a residuary clause. Property escheats (that is, it goes to the state government) after passing through intestacy when no intestate heirs can be ascertained. A residuary clause is a good way to avoid the undesirable prospect of estate assets falling into the coffers of the state government.

Rights of the Surviving Spouse

In most states the spouse of the decedent is protected from being disinherited. So, if the surviving spouse is left out of the will, or is only given a nominal share of the estate, that spouse may have the option of taking under the deceased spouse's will or renouncing the will and taking an "elective share" of the estate. An elective share is that portion of the estate that the surviving spouse is entitled to receive by state statute, regardless of the testator's wishes. The elective share will generally be one third to one half of the estate, depending on what state one is in and whether any children are surviving. This right of election however, may be contracted away by the spouses in the form of a prenuptial or post-nuptial agreement. Also, the laws of each state may provide ways of avoiding a spouse's outright elective share entitlement. For example, in New York State, if a decedent has bequeathed to his or her spouse the sum of $10,000 outright and has placed the rest of the value of the elective share in trust for the surviving spouse, with an indefeasible right to the income thereon for life, the surviving spouse would have no outright right of election.

The rationale for providing this "elective" option

is that contribution by the surviving spouse to the decedent's ability to acquire wealth during their marriage, and therefore, the surviving spouse is entitled to at least a portion of it.

Important when considering the elective share statute in one's state is what exactly the divisible estate consists of. Given the proliferation of testamentary substitutes, many assets that would have once passed through probate may now be severed from the estate prior to probate and placed in trust or joint tenancy. Both the Uniform Probate Code and the laws of many states provide that a surviving spouse can enforce their elective rights on many types of testamentary substitutes in order to calculate their elective share. In these states, testamentary substitutes such as inter vivos trusts (where the donor retains any interest) and joint tenancy accounts will be included in the estate for elective share calculations.

A growing number of states use what is known as a "community property" system. This system is premised on the belief that everything acquired during the marriage belongs equally (fifty-fifty) to each spouse. However, property belonging to each spouse before the marriage is considered the separate property of each spouse respectively and thus is not subject to equal division upon death or divorce.

RIGHTS OF THE CHILDREN

In almost every state a child or other lineal descendant has no statutory protection from being disinherited by a parent. If one wishes to leave a child nothing, or a minimal amount, it is usually advisable to specifically state so. In general, disinheriting a child is not favored by law, especially when there is no surviving spouse. There is always the possibility of a court's using its equitable powers to allow a child at least to get their intestate share of the parent's estate. The rationale in this type of situation is that otherwise it may be financially unfair or injurious to the child, especially if there is no surviving parent and/or the child is a minor.

ABATEMENT

Abatement will be necessary when your estate does not have sufficient assets to pay all the debts of the estate and all the bequests as well. This situation can be created by unexpected estate taxes or other unknown contingencies that may drain the estate. When this occurs, some of the bequests will be abated (eliminated or reduced). In the absence of instructions in the will, bequests will usually abate as follows: residuary bequests will be reduced first; general legacies which are usually cash bequests are reduced second; specific legacies which are dispositions of specific items, are abated last, and can be prorated.

ADEMPTION

Ademption is when a specifically bequeathed item of property is no longer in the testator's estate at the time of death. An example of this would be if a certain

automobile is bequeathed to an heir but before the
testator's death it is sold and a different car is purchased. If the will is not updated to reflect the change
the bequest will fail because you cannot gift to another
something you do not have. If the bequest had been
more general, like leaving all cars owned at death,
then the beneficiary would receive the different car.

One should consult one's own state's laws in order
to plan bequests and devises properly so as to be
aware of and to try to avoid abatement or ademption
problems.

A good way to approach the task of beneficiary
selection is to first make a list of family members,
close relatives, friends, and any other people or organizations who will share in the estate. The next stop is
to assess the priority of each prospective beneficiary
and consider any special needs they may have that
should be addressed. After the list of prospective
beneficiaries has been compiled, an accurate accounting of all assets and liabilities of the estate should be
prepared. Determine the actual distributions to each
beneficiary in a way that closely fits one's intentions
and satisfies any legal obligations. Remember, some
assets will be suitable only for certain beneficiaries.
For example, one may not want to leave a high-
maintenance item, such as a boat or a plane, to a
person with little cash on hand.

After completing a tentative distribution sched-
ule, each bequest should be examined to determine its
overall validity, which should be based on applicable
distribution restrictions and tax consequences, both
federal and state. In many instances there will be
ways to pass real or personal property to an intended
beneficiary without having to go through the probate

or administrative maze, or pay estate taxes. It is advisable to seek professional advice regarding the overall distribution strategy, the validity of bequests and devises, and the viable alternatives that may exist.

CHAPTER VI

AVOIDANCE OF PROBATE

Probate can be avoided by creating property owner-ships during one's lifetime, so that on death such property will pass to heirs through separate survivor-ship arrangements rather than through probate. This process may reduce the costs of the administration of an estate and possibly lower estate taxes.

Examples of this kind of property ownerships are trusts, (revocable and irrevocable), life-insurance policies, joint accounts, gifts, annuities, joint tenancies, and pension and retirement benefits. Transfers such as these are, in most instances, are for tax purposes considered incomplete because the owner is able to change the arrangement.

It is important to point out that in many cases the

reduction in the probate costs for administering these types of assets may be less than the costs of creating and administering them during one's lifetime. Trusts that are revocable for transfer tax purposes provide no tax savings whatsoever. Jointly owned property will normally pass to the surviving owner outside of one's will, but for estate tax purposes the gross estate of a decedent will include the value of property held jointly at the time of death. However, that part of the joint property owned by another person will not be included, and if the survivor is the spouse of the decedent, only one–half of the value will be included, notwithstanding the amount contributed to the joint asset by either spouse.

LIFE INSURANCE AND BANK ACCOUNTS

In many situations the issue arises as to whether a beneficiary of a life insurance policy can be changed by a will. A majority of states hold that where the policy requires that a written notice of change of beneficiary be filed with the insurance company, the beneficiary of a life insurance policy may not be changed by a will.

The Uniform Probate Code holds that during one's lifetime a joint account belongs proportionally to each contributor; thus, a depositor of such an account can revoke the joint ownership at any time. Under the laws of the State of New York each joint owner has the right to one–half of the joint account.

Under the Uniform Probate Code, a spouse-joint owner is entitled to the balance of the joint account upon the death of the spouse, unless there is clear and convincing evidence of a different intention at the time the account is created. The majority of states hold that

the surviving joint owner is entitled to the entire
account, unless mental incapacity, undue influence,
fraud, or mistake is shown. The laws of some states
hold that there is a presumption of survivorship rights
in favor of the surviving owner.

Bank accounts may be created that prevent the
other joint owner from withdrawing any funds before
the creator's death. During the creator's lifetime the
beneficiary of such an account normally has no rights
to the account, and is entitled to such funds only after
the death of the depositor. If the beneficiary of such an
account should predecease the creator, an account of
this kind would pass under the residuary clause of the
will of the depositor. In the state of New York, these
accounts are commonly called Totten Trust Accounts.
The creation of a joint interest may subject such a
transfer to gift tax.

Revocable or living trusts are the most important
devices used in estate plans managed by large banks.
A trust of this nature is an inter vivos creation in
which the settlor retains the right to revoke or amend
the agreement, in whole or in part. Generally, the
settlor is the beneficiary of the trust during his or her
lifetime. The revocable trust is a will substitute and
normally provides that upon the settlor's death it
becomes irrevocable, and therefore it contains dispositive provisions that will take effect upon the death of
the settlor.

However, as a part of the estate plan, the settlor
will need to execute, together with the trust, a
pour-over will, which transfers to the trust any assets
still owned by the settlor at the time of death. These
assets will be added to the assets of the trust and
administered as an integral part.

In addition to the avoidance of probate and a reduction in administration costs, this type of plan offers the settlor privacy, as probate files are generally open to public view.

There are no estate tax savings in the creation of this kind of trust. The settlor, by reserving the power over the property for tax purposes, is considered to be the owner. As such, the balance of the revocable trust at the time of the creator's death will be included in the estate for estate-transfer tax purposes.

A funded revocable trust will afford the creator with an opportunity to view exactly how the trust operates. It can provide a vehicle for other family members to make gifts either while they are alive or through their own testamentary plans. And a trust that is created and is actually in operation while one is still alive is less likely to be attacked on the basis of fraud or undue influence or a lack of capacity on the part of the settlor.

CHAPTER VII

TRUSTS

A trust is a legal entity that can be created to serve a wide array of financial planning needs. The written trust instrument allows the owner of property to transfer the benefits of that property to others while leaving legal ownership of the property in the trust. The property interests created in trusts may be considered gifts and are therefore subject to gift tax.

Trusts can be created to serve numerous functions. They can be used to separate the responsibility of ownership from the benefits of ownership of certain property; to avoid or decrease federal income and estate taxes; or to provide steady and controlled support for minors, incompetents, and other dependents. To understand how a trust works one must first become familiar with some basic terms and the necessary requirements for establishing a trust.

THE SETTLOR (DONOR/ GRANTOR)

The person that transfers property into the trust is known as the settlor. Generally this is the person that decides to create the trust. The settlor determines what property goes into the trust, the purpose of the trust, who are the trustees, who are the beneficiaries, how long the trust should last, and how the trust funds are to be utilized.

THE TRUSTEE

The person or institution that holds legal title to the assets transferred to the trust is known as the trustee. The trust exists exclusively for the benefit of the beneficiary, with the trustee being its fiduciary holder, responsible for the management of the trust assets, keeping them separate and accounted for. The trustee is paid a fee or commission and receives no benefit from the trust, unless also a beneficiary. A trust may have one or more individual trustees, or the trustee may be an individual or a corporation. Usually, the trustee is appointed by the settlor; however, if the settlor fails to designate an original or successor trustee, the courts will name a trustee and the trust will generally be valid. However, neither the courts nor the settlor may force a person to be trustee, and the trustee must consent to the appointment.

Selecting a competent and responsible trustee is

extremely important. The trustee will be responsible
for carrying out the intentions of the settlor as ex-
pressed in the trust instrument; so the trustee must
be honest, willing and able. The trustee must also be
qualified to handle all the management, financial, and
accounting duties necessary to properly administer
the trust, so a trustee with professional knowledge is
advisable.

THE BENEFICIARY

The beneficiary is a person, or group of persons, who
hold equitable title to the trust and receive the benefits from it. An income beneficiary is entitled to any
income the trust may earn. The remainderman is also
a beneficiary, and is entitled to the principal after the
entitlement for the income beneficiary terminates, as
provided under the terms of the trust instrument. If
trust assets are mismanaged the remainderman in
addition to the income beneficiary, can have a personal
claim against the trustee.

Income beneficiaries and remainder beneficiaries
will generally have conflicting investment desires with
regard to the use of the trust property, given the
nature of their interests. The income beneficiary will
normally seek to receive as high a return as possible in
order to maximize the trust's current income. In order
to gain these higher rates of return, the trust property
will be subject to a greater risk of being lost. Income
beneficiaries will be more willing to take such risks if
they do not have an interest in the principal itself. The
main goal of the remainderman, on the other hand,
will be to preserve and protect the principal. Accord-

ingly, the remainderman will want the trust to invest in lower-yielding, lower-risk investments. The trustee must equally balance the interests of the income beneficiary and the remainderman in order to fulfill fiduciary obligations. Trustees, therefore, have a high degree of legal responsibility to the beneficiaries of a trust. They have, in most instances, the obligations of obtaining a reasonable income for the income beneficiary and a reasonable appreciation of the value of its assets for those who will eventually receive those benefits.

The property that the settlor transfers into the trust is known as the "corpus" or "principal." It may be transferred in different ways, depending on the nature of the property. If the trust property is "personal property," such as stock, then either actual delivery or a deed is required. If the trust property is "real property," such as land, then a written instrument transferring it to the trust will be needed. (Mere intent to put property into a trust will not suffice.)

SETTING UP THE TRUST

There are three formal requirements for setting up a trust. Keep in mind that the main purpose of these requirements is simply to provide certainty and to avoid confusion.

The settlor must manifest the intention to create a trust relationship. Thus, a trust arrangement may not be inferred or assumed, and the settlor must take some affirmative action which illustrates that intent. There must also be trust property; a trust cannot exist without a corpus or principal. Any type of property such as contingent remainders, life-insurance policies, or even leasehold interests will suffice. Finally, there must also be one or more trust beneficiaries. These beneficiaries, in some cases, may be unborn, but they must be ascertained. If there are no beneficiaries then the trust benefits no one, and thus serves no purpose. Problems may arise when it cannot be determined who the beneficiaries of a trust are because of vagueness. If there are no designated beneficiaries and the trustees are not entitled to declare the beneficiaries of their choice, the trust may fail. The specific power of beneficiary selection may be granted by the settlor in the trust instrument. However, to ensure that all wishes are carried out the settlor should make these selections.

The legal and equitable aspects of trust ownership may be created either by an inter vivos trust or a testamentary trust.

INTER VIVOS TRUST

An inter vivos trust is a trust agreement made while the settlor is still alive, and it is irrevocable unless the trust instrument specifically states to the contrary. A trust of this kind may be created in one of two ways. The settlor may simple declare the holding of personal property for the benefit of another, which is known as a "declaration of trust," whereupon the settlor is the trustee. Alternatively, the settlor may transfer title in property to a trustee for the benefit of the settlor or another person. The inter vivos trust may be revocable or irrevocable, depending upon state laws and the language of the trust instrument. Some states require that if a trust is to be revocable there must be specific language in the instrument stating so. It is extremely important to consult the applicable state laws before setting up any type of trust.

The inter vivos trust can have tax advantages, as this type of trust can allow a shifting of income from one person to another. For example, if one wanted to provide another with the income generated by interest earned on cash or the dividends of a certain stock, the owner would have to take the interest or dividends as taxable income and then give the after-tax amount to the intended person. If, on the other hand, the property had been placed into a trust, the recipient, now a trust beneficiary, might pay less in taxes. The trust would serve as a flow-through entity allowing the income to pass to the beneficiary.

The amount of control the settlor or transferor retains over the inter vivos trust can raise questions regarding intent and, thus, the validity of the trust. In all jurisdictions, the validity of a trust where the settlor maintains the right to revoke the trust during lifetime is accepted. However, where the settlor is the trustee and the sole beneficiary of the trust, and no valid trust intent can be found, the courts in some jurisdictions have invalidated the arrangement. Generally, as long as some interest is created in at least a beneficiary other than the settlor, the trust will be valid even though the settlor retains extensive powers. One should note that the settlor and spouse of the settlor are considered the same person.

TESTAMENTARY TRUST

A testamentary trust is one which is created by a will. In this instance the transfer of the corpus in trust becomes effective only at the death of the settlor, and only a valid will can create a testamentary trust of either real or personal property. These trusts will sometimes be called "court trusts" because they are administered by the probate court.

States that follow the Uniform Probate Code will require the trustee to register the trust with the court in the principal place of administration. The registration will identify the settlor, the trustees, and the beneficiaries.

The pour-over will function as a way to merge inter vivos trust assets with testamentary trust assets. If one sets up a trust during one's lifetime they may, either concurrently or thereafter, provide a pour-over clause in their will, which permits certain probate assets to become part of the trust. The idea of the pour-over is to allow assets of the testamentary estate, insurance proceeds, and other assets to be pooled together into one fund.

Legislatures in every state have enacted statutes permitting a will to pour-over estate assets into an inter vivos trust on the date of death. There is also the Uniform Testamentary Additions to Trusts Act, which provides that when probate assets are poured-over into an inter vivos trust they become part of the inter vivos trust.

SUPPORTING DEPENDENTS

A testamentary trust can provide an excellent way to support dependents, family members, and important others. The advantage of the testamentary trust over an outright bequest or devise through a will is that the settlor of the trust maintains control over the property through the trust instrument, even after death. This can be very important for numerous reasons.

There are many situations where a beneficiary may be incapable of handling the responsibility of maintaining or managing the property that has been left to them. The beneficiary could be a minor, incompetent, or just plain irresponsible. In many cases it would be a disaster to transfer large amounts of cash or complex investment portfolios to someone inexperienced in handling such assets. The danger of these assets being lost through mismanagement or overindulgence on the part of the beneficiary could be great. By having these types of properties placed into a trust, the management and distribution functions are carried out by the trustee according to the trust instrument.

For example, let's say one wishes to leave $100,000 to each of two children, ages seventeen and twenty-one. More likely than not, neither child will have experience in handling such large amounts of cash. If this is the case, $100,000 may seem like an inexhaustible fortune until two or three years down the road when it could all be gone. The hard-earned financial cushion one sought to provide for their children would then be lost. However, there are numerous types of trusts that can be used to create certain distribution restrictions, which will ensure a longer-term preservation of the trust assets.

TYPES OF TRUSTS

The Support Trust

As the settlor of a support trust, one may provide in the trust instrument that the beneficiaries are only to receive as much of the income or principal as is necessary to support and educate them. This will ensure that the funds left behind will be used to provide for the beneficiaries in a sensible manner. Although the corpus of the trust may be invaded as necessary if the trusts instrument contains such provision, it will also be controlled by necessity, not by the whim or desire of the beneficiary.

The Discretionary Trust

The discretionary trust places more responsibility upon the trustee regarding distribution of income and principal. Under this type of trust, the trustee may distribute to a beneficiary as much income or principal as the trustee deems proper. Generally, a trustee will have great freedom to determine distributions. However, the trustee may not shirk the fiduciary obligations required under the trust instrument by distributing the funds improperly. In some instances, an equity court may step in to control a trustee in the exercise of fiduciary discretion if there has been a failure to observe the intent of the testator. Improper distributions might be those favoring one beneficiary over another, unreasonably refusing to distribute assets, or failing to adequately provide for the beneficiaries according to the testator's intent. However, in this type of trust the trustee can be given the discretionary right to distribute the benefits of the trust to or for the benefit of a number of beneficiaries. This is often called a "sprinkling" or "spray" provision in a trust and under such clause a trustee can make distributions to the beneficiaries without regard to equality.

The Spendthrift Trust

A spendthrift trust imposes a restraint upon the equitable interest of the beneficiary in the trust. A spendthrift is a person who is incapable of managing assets prudently, so essentially, this type of trust prevents beneficiaries from selling or losing their interest in the trust to others. It imposes a disabling restraint on the beneficiaries and creditors: the beneficiaries cannot voluntarily transfer their interests, and their creditors cannot reach their interests. Courts have generally permitted settlors to qualify the interests they are giving in trust in this manner. In New York State, all trusts are considered spendthrift unless the settlor expressly makes the beneficiaries' interest transferable with certain statutory exceptions. The Uniform Probate Code works the opposite way: a trust is not considered spendthrift unless the settlor expressly makes the beneficiaries' interests nontransferable.

The Charitable Trust

Charitable trusts may be either inter vivos or testamentary in nature and may be set up to elect charities as either income and/or remainder beneficiaries. For a charitable trust to be valid it must serve some charitable purpose. Legitimate purposes include, but are not limited to, certain types of assistance for the financially disadvantaged, and to advance a social interest of society, or assistance to help legally bring about a change in the law. The size of the group designated to benefit from the trust may vary. However, the larger the group of beneficiaries the more flexibility there is.

One of the great differences between a charitable and noncharitable trust is that the former is not subject to the rule against perpetuities which rule is discussed later on in this book. This means that charitable trust arrangements may be perpetually in existence, depending on whether or not the trust is for the income or the remainder of the trust property. Explanations of several types of charitable trusts are as follows:

The Charitable Remainder Annuity Trust

An annuity trust pays a fixed annual sum to the noncharitable income beneficiary without regard to current income yields of the trust. The amount to be received should not be less than 5 percent of the original value of the trust in order to preserve certain tax benefits to the creator of the trust. The present value of the donee's remainder interest in the charitable remainder that may qualify under certain conditions is a charitable deduction to the donor for federal income, gift, and estate tax purposes. The amount of the deduction would be less if the gift provides for a successor individual beneficiary to receive a benefit from the trust before the charity receives the remainder interest after the first beneficiary's death.

The annuity trust provides the income beneficiary with the greatest protection against loss in the value of the trust's principal. The beneficiary is not at the mercy of the market or general economic fluctuations, since the fixed amount of the annuity must be paid even if the corpus of the trust must be consumed to satisfy the commitment.

The Charitable Remainder Unitrust

A charitable remainder unitrust pays out each year an amount generally equal to a fixed percentage (at least 5 percent), as selected by the donor, of the value of trust assets for the tax year. The trust assets are usually valued, as provided in the trust agreement, on the first business day of each taxable year.

This type of trust may also be designed to pay out either its net income for the year, or the specified fixed percentage amount, whichever is less. This arrangement is commonly called a "net income" unitrust. With a net income unitrust, the trust agreement may provide that for the years in which trust income exceeds the specified unitrust amount, the excess income may be used to make up for past years, in which the trust's net income was less than that amount. This type of net income unitrust is known as one with a "make-up" or "catch-up" provision.

The charitable remainder unitrust has the benefit of providing a hedge against inflation. In an inflationary economy, the value of the trusts assets should increase along with prices in general, thus providing higher annual payments to the income beneficiary; on the other hand, when the market in general is down, the payments decrease.

This trust is also flexible, since it can receive additional transfers of property subsequent to the initial transfer. Therefore, the same trust can be used for multiple charitable gifts, thus eliminating the costs of creating multiple trusts.

A possible disadvantage of the unitrust is the uncertainty of the amount of the annual payment to the income beneficiary. Accordingly, a donor whose primary concern is the certainty of the amount of income distributed to the income beneficiary should not utilize the unitrust for making a charitable remainder gift.

The Charitable Lead Trust

The charitable lead trust is similar in many ways to the charitable remainder trust. As a result of charitable deductions these trusts are vehicles used to transfer substantial amounts of wealth from generation to generation largely free of estate and gift taxes. Under this trust agreement an annuity or unitrust amount is paid to a nonprofit organization for a term of years or for the life of an individual. On the termination of the lead trust, the trust assets either revert to the donor or are distributed to others (usually heirs).

MODIFICATIONS OF TRUSTS

Generally, courts will be reluctant to modify the distributive provisions of an irrevocable trust instrument. However, in order to prevent impairment of a settlor's primary purpose, permission to deviate from the express terms of the trust may be granted by the court. When a trustee or beneficiary petitions the court to invade the corpus or accumulated income for support, or in some other way to change the distribution scheme, usually all of the beneficiaries must consent or the court will most likely deny it.

In general, charitable trust schemes may not be altered unless the purpose of the trust has become illegal or impossible to perform.

TERMINATION OF TRUSTS

A trust will normally provide in its organizational document when it will terminate. The ability to terminate an existing trust, in contravention to its stated term, will to a large degree depend on whether or not the settlor is still alive. In an inter vivos trust if the settlor and all of the beneficiaries consent and all beneficiaries are adult and competent a trust may be terminated and the trustee, if not an interested party, may not object to this action. The right to do this exists regardless of any existing or implied spendthrift clause. If the settlor is not living a trust cannot

be terminated prior to the time fixed for termination
in the trust instrument (even though all beneficiaries
consent), if termination would be contrary to the
material purpose of the settlor. The courts will seek to
preserve the wishes of the settlor to the greatest
extent possible. Many state laws vary with regard to
permitting the termination of trusts. It is wise to
check your own state law in this area.

TAXATION OF TRUSTS

Trusts and estates are types of income-producing
entities the Internal Revenue Code recognizes. Prior
to the present relatively flat tax rates, trusts were
often used as income-splitting devices by those in the
higher tax brackets to shift money to a lower tax
bracket. The typical scheme was to distribute income-
producing assets to a spouse or child in trust, and the
spouse or child in a lower tax bracket would pay less in
taxes. The savings could be quite significant if one
spouse was in the 50 percent tax bracket and the other
was in the 20 to 30 percent tax bracket. However, the
flattening of individual tax rates to 15 percent and 28
percent, and the corporate rates to 15 percent, 25
percent, and 34 percent, have largely reduced the
incentives for income-splitting between spouses. Furthermore, since the top marginal income tax rate of 31
percent applies to trust's or estate's undistributed
income at very low levels there is no real income tax
incentive to accumulate income in trusts. The "kiddie
tax," imposed by the 1986 Tax Reform Act, taxes, at
the higher parent's rate, a child's unearned income
over $1,000, if the child is under the age of fourteen,

and has at least one living parent. This has eliminated any incentive to shift income to a child.

THE GRANTOR TRUST

A grantor trust is one in which the income is taxable to the settlor because the settlor retains substantial control over the trust assets or retains certain prohibited administrative powers. An example of this would be a revocable inter vivos trust. By retaining the power of revocation, the settlor can terminate the trust at any time and reclaim the trust assets. When the purpose of setting up the trust is to benefit the settlor directly or indirectly, and the settlor has control or advantage with regard to the trust assets, the settlor is taxed on the trust income.

The Internal Revenue Code determines the extent of the settlor's interest in the trust by what is called the "5 percent Rule." Where the grantor/settlor has a reversionary interest in either the corpus or the income of all or any part of the trust assets, and this interest exceeds 5 percent of all or a part of the value of the trust's assets, the trust is considered a grantor trust for federal tax purposes. Therefore, the trust income is taxable to the settlor. The 5 percent valuation is based on the fair-market value of the reversionary interest at the time the trust is created.

CHAPTER VIII

LIMITING FUTURE INTERESTS

FUTURE INTERESTS

A future interest is a nonpossessory interest that may become possessory in the future. For instance, one may leave all of their property to X for life, and when X dies, the remainder of the property is to pass to Y. However, Y has no right to possess or enjoy X's property in the present. Further, if X spends or uses up all of the property, then when X dies, Y would have an interest in nothing. Future interests generally arise through some type of trust arrangement or through a will. Also, these interests may be sold, given away, or seized by creditors.

There are numerous types of future interests

which may be created, depending on either the nature of the property or the intent of the creator.

When real property is involved a possessory estate is known as a "fee simple absolute." This is an estate that has the potential of enduring forever; and it can endure forever because land will generally endure forever. The fee simple absolute constitutes absolute ownership of infinite duration. If one has a fee simple absolute to a certain piece of land, that means that no competing future interest exists in that land. If, however, one's interest in the land may be cut short or terminated at some time in the future, it becomes a defeasible fee, meaning that a future interest in the estate exists. The defeasible fee may be either a fee simple determinable or a fee simple subject to a condition subsequent. The fee simple determinable will terminate automatically on the happening of a given event such as the cessuation of occupying and residence on the land. The fee simple subject to a condition subsequent will create an optional right to retake the property.

Another type of future interest is known as the life estate. This is an estate that will necessarily end at the death of the person to whom the life estate has been given. A life estate is created when one leaves property to someone for their life, and then to someone else upon their death.

A reversion is a retained interest which is created by the person who is making the transfer. In this situation the transferor gives away only some of the rights in the property, while retaining others. It may help to imagine property rights as a bundle of straws which together form the entire rights to the property.

A reversion is created by giving away less than the full bundle of rights being held.

A remainder is a future interest which can become possessory on the termination of all prior interests in the property. One literally gets what remains of the interest in the property.

THE RULE AGAINST PERPETUITIES

When the disposition of property is at issue there is a rule which must be complied with in most states known as the Rule Against Perpetuities. This rule was established centuries ago to insure that large amounts of land and wealth could not be tied up indefinitely in the hands of a few. This rule also prevents a trust from existing forever. The rule provides that every present or future interest in property shall be void, at inception, if the interest created in the property by the transferor will suspend the absolute power of disposition by a longer period than lives in being at the time of the creation of the interest plus a stated term of years (determined by each state).

Therefore, usually under the rule it is compulsory to terminate a testamentary trust at the end of a certain period of time measured by those who are alive at the time of the testator's death plus a period of time.

Given the possible contingencies and complexities involved with future interests and the Rule Against Perpetuities one should seek professional help in drafting such interests.

CHAPTER IX

ESTATE TAXATION

FEDERAL TAXATION

The federal government imposes an estate tax upon the transfer of a decedent's property. This tax is paid by the estate of the decedent and not by the beneficiary of the property. Furthermore, the federal government will normally receive its tax payment before beneficiaries receive their respective shares of the estate.

The federal estate tax is the most expensive tax we have. The top rate is now 55 percent, and on January 1, 1993 it will drop to 50 percent. Individuals with large estates can be subject to an additional 5 percent surtax, which applies to estates having a value between $10

million and $21 million. Therefore, the highest estate tax
enforced at these levels is 60 percent.

Under the federal tax code, many estates will be
exempt from paying any federal estate taxes. Since
1987, the Tax Code has permitted a tax exemption on
the first $600,000 of the value of the estate, commonly
called the "Unified Credit." Therefore, if your estate is
valued below $600,000, you will not have any federal
estate tax liability, if no taxable transfers were made
during lifetime. Furthermore, under what is known as
the "unlimited marital deduction," a spouse can die,
leaving the entire estate to the surviving spouse, and
there is no federal tax regardless of the estate value.

Since the federal gift and estate tax systems were
unified under the Tax Reform Act of 1976, taxable
lifetime gifts may increase the death taxes an estate
may have to pay and will reduce the availability of the
Unified Credit at the time of death.

Since January 1, 1987, the Unified Credit is equal
to $192,800 in tax, and directly reduces the amount of
taxes an estate is required to pay. If an individual does
not make any taxable gifts during their lifetime, the
entire credit will be available at the time of death.

When a person has a spouse an estate plan should
be created that makes the maximum use of the Unified
Credit and the unlimited marital deduction. A marital
deduction is permitted under the federal tax code where
any part of a deceased person's estate passes to a surviving spouse. Under the federal estate tax law, an
estate is entitled to a marital deduction for a transfer of
property to a trust for the benefit of a spouse, if the
property so transferred meets the requirements of a
"qualified terminable interest property," and an election
is made to treat the property as such on the estate tax
return.

MAXIMUM FEDERAL CREDIT FOR
ESTATE DEATH TAXES

Amount on Which Tentative Federal Tax Is Computed	Tentative Federal Tax Before Credits: Tax and % on Next Block		Federal Estate Tax Maximum Credit for State Inheritance Tax Amount and % on Next Block	
$	$	18 %	$	%
10,000	1,800	20		
20,000	3,800	22		
40,000	8,200	24		
50,000	10,600	24		
60,000	13,000	26		
80,000	18,200	28		
100,000	23,800	30		0.8
150,000	38,800	32	400	1.6
200,000	54,800	32	1,200	2.4
250,000	70,800	34	2,400	2.4
300,000	87,800	34	3,600	3.2
500,000	155,800	37	10,000	4.0
700,000	229,800	37	18,000	4.8
750,000	248,300	39	20,400	4.8
900,000	306,800	39	27,600	5.6
1,000,000	345,800	41	33,200	5.6
1,100,000	386,800	41	38,800	6.4
1,250,000	448,300	43	48,400	6.4
1,500,000	555,800	45	64,400	6.4
1,600,000	600,800	45	70,800	7.2
2,000,000	780,800	49	99,600	7.2
2,100,000	829,800	49	106,800	8.0
2,500,000	1,025,800	53	138,800	8.0
2,600,000	1,078,800	53	146,800	8.8
3,000,000	1,290,800	55	182,000	8.8
3,100,000	1,345,800	55	190,800	9.6
3,500,000	1,565,800	55	229,200	9.6
3,600,000	1,620,800	55	238,800	10.4
4,000,000	1,840,800	55	280,400	10.4
4,100,000	1,895,800	55	290,800	11.2
4,500,000	2,115,800	55	335,600	11.2
5,000,000	2,390,800	55	391,600	11.2
6,100,000	2,445,800	55	402,800	12.0
7,100,000	3,434,800	55	522,800	12.8
8,100,000	4,095,800	55	786,700	14.4
9,100,000	4,645,800	55	930,800	15.2
10,100,000	5,195,800	55	1,082,200	16.0

The term "qualified terminable interest property" means property that passes from the decedent and in which the remaining spouse has a qualifying income interest for life. A surviving spouse will have a qualifying income interest for life if that person is entitled to all the income from the property, and the property may not be transferred to any other persons during the spouse's lifetime.

In addition to the Unified Credit, additional credits may be deducted from the gross estate tax, to determine the estate tax payable. These are:

1. credit for state death taxes;
2. credit for gift taxes;
3. credit for tax on prior transfers;
4. credit for foreign death taxes.

Under the current federal tax code, if a person dies and if the gross estate of that person is more than $600,000, a federal estate tax return must be filed. The return is due nine months after the date of death of an individual, unless an extension of time to file the same has been approved. Any estate tax due under this return is required to be paid with the filing of the return. There are various provisions under the federal code permitting additional time to pay the estate tax.

There are two methods to value the assets of a decedent. One method values the assets as of the date of death of the decedent. The other is the alternate valuation method, which values the assets as of a date other than the date of death. Currently, the alternate valuation date is a date six months after the decedent's date of death. The rationale behind the alternate valuation method is the ability of the estate to reduce its tax liability if the value of the property of the estate has decreased since the date of the decedent's death.

Under federal tax law, there is an exemption for each individual of up to $1 million, applicable to generation-skipping transfers. This transfer is defined as a transfer of property by a person to an individual at least two generations younger than the transferor. Transfers of this kind are subject to this tax whether they are given outright or placed in trust.

The generating-skipping tax is a separate tax imposed at a flat rate of 50 percent, and it is a tax payable in addition to the estate tax. This tax is based upon the fair-market value of the property transferred, subject to the allowable deductions, exemptions, and credits.

For estates of non–resident aliens, the federal estate tax law applies the same rates beginning at 18 percent on the first $10,000 of taxable transfers, reaching 55 percent on taxable transfers over $3 million. For estates of decedents dying after November 10, 1988, no marital deduction is allowed for property passing to a surviving spouse who is not a United States citizen. But, a marital deduction will be allowed for property passing to a surviving alien spouse if the property is placed in a domestic qualified trust (or QDT). In order to qualify as a QDT, among other things, the alien spouse must receive all of the income from the trust and the trust must meet all of the applicable Treasury Department requirements.

STATE ESTATE TAXATION

Almost every state taxes in some form the transfer of wealth associated with estate distribution. Unlike federal estate taxes, most states do not tax the estate directly; instead, states place a tax upon the recipient of the estate property. This type of tax is called an inheritance tax, and the amount of this tax will vary greatly from state to state. The inheritance tax will also vary based on who is receiving the decedent's property, how much they are receiving, and what their relationship is to the decedent.

Some states, such as New York, have gone as far as creating their own estate tax. Although an estate may not incur a federal estate tax liability by not exceeding the Unified Credit amount, state inheritance taxes may still be due. Although there is usually an exemption amount at the state estate tax level, on average it is much lower than the Unified Credit exemption at the federal level. Therefore, even the smallest estate may be subject to state transfer taxes.

The various types of tax imposed by the states on estates can be categorized into three classes: (1) an inheritance tax is applied by approximately eighteen states on the basis of the family relationship of the beneficiary to the decedent and the amount of the inheritance; (2) a pick-up or sponge tax, which in approximately twenty-eight states is the only death tax imposed, and which means that unless the estate is subject to federal estate tax there will be no death taxes paid to these jurisdictions; (3) an estate tax, currently imposed in approximately six states, which is a transfer tax imposed on the entire estate in the same fashion that the federal estate tax is applied, but at different (lower) rates.

Generally, transfers to the surviving spouse of a decedent are transfer-tax free.

The federal estate tax rates are much higher than those charged by the states, and planning should center around the impact of this tax.

Multiple states can impose transfer taxes on the same property, so the most important estate planning that one should do to avoid these problems is to be sure that their permanent residence, or domicile, is clarified.

CHAPTER X

ESTATE PLANNING AFTER DEATH

Estate planning does not stop at death. Postmortem planning is necessary to achieve (1) the optimum estate and income tax savings for both the estate and its beneficiaries; (2) the modification of the estate plan of the decedent by the application of disclaimers or renunciations in order to reduce the impact of estate taxes.

It is possible to achieve tax savings based upon the timing of distributions. The use of a renunciation or a disclaimer can result in the transference of distributions from one who has a beneficial interest under a will to another person, hopefully without the imposition of any gift taxes. There are tax-planning options and goals that should be applied as well, such as a sprinkling of the income of the estate among the greatest number of beneficiaries so that the split income is taxed at perhaps lower rates than if it is distributed to fewer individuals. Furthermore, payments from the estate may be postponed if the income tax brackets of the beneficiary and the estate are different. An estate can opt for an income tax year that is different from the beneficiary's so that the beneficiary may defer taxation of the estate's income. This procedure can provide the estate with deductions for a particular tax year and, for income tax purposes, the beneficiary will not be required to report the income until a later year. In order to be in a position to avail the estate and the beneficiaries of these possibilities, the fiduciary should know all of the financial details of the estate (i.e., what the income of the estate will be) and must be sure that the estate has the liquidity to carry out these objectives.

The executor of the estate has the right to elect on the estate tax return, that is, to treat certain property of the estate as qualified terminable interest property (commonly known as Q-tip), which can qualify for a marital deduction if the conditions of the regulations are met. This selection can be made by the executor notwithstanding the absence of any provisions in the will to so do. Such an election must be timely and made in accordance with the regulations.

A disclaimer or a renunciation is a useful tool in postmortem planning. Traditionally, persons who receive property from an estate are thrilled to receive a windfall. However, sometimes a beneficiary may have a good reason to refuse such a gift, such as the ability of the estate to take advantage of the tax laws and thereby increase the after tax value of the estate. This can be accomplished by disclaiming or renouncing the particular property interest. By doing so, the benefit in question will normally pass to a person entitled to it under the laws of the state involved. Disclaimers, in order to be proper, have to meet the requirements of certain federal regulations, as well as the laws of the particular state where the estate is located. States also have provisions governing the distribution of property that is renounced. Usually under state statutes, such property will go to those individuals who would have inherited the property had the disclaimant died before the decedent. A minority of states provide that a disclaimer will increase the shares of the residuary legatees. Postmortem planning for business interests requires some familiarity with the applicable tax rules.

Additionally, certain elections are available that permit an executor to elect to have a farm or business property valued (for estate tax purposes) on the basis of its special use as a farm or business property, rather than on the basis of its highest and best use. The requirements of the regulations covering these matters must be met if such an election is to be made. If it is a farm, this special election will be of value only where the farming land is not presently, or in the foreseeable future, the highest and best use. If the property is located in a sparsely populated agricultural area, farming is likely to be the highest and best use. If the property is located in an area which presently, or in the near future, may be developed for residential, commercial or other purposes, the election will take on a special meaning.

An executor/administrator is required to exercise the diligence that the ordinarily prudent person would exercise in their own affairs. A professional executor/administrator, such as an institution, may even be held to a higher standard of diligence.

CHAPTER XI

BUSINESS PLANNING

Upon the sudden death of an owner of a business, the value of the business interest must be ascertained, a process which can be difficult at any time. To avoid disputes, litigation, and (sometimes) divisiveness, buy/sell agreements are very often entered into by the owners. Among other things, buy/sell agreements provide for the remaining or surviving owners to purchase the interest of an estate in the business, usually according to a specified or predetermined formula. In many instances, insurance is purchased by the owners on each others' lives to fund such a buy-out. A properly drafted agreement of this kind can insure that the ownership of a business is not transferred outside a specified group. Such an agreement can afford the continuity of management by the surviving shareholders. In addition, it can cover the sale of the interest of a shareholder who sustains a permanent disability and as a result cannot contribute service to the business. This kind of agreement normally also provides for the transfer of a retiring shareholder's interest in the company to the remaining shareholders.

One of the important estate-planning benefits from a buy/sell arrangement is the setting of a value of the decedent's interest in a business for estate-tax purposes. The federal taxing authorities will normally accept such valuations provided they are created on an arm's-length basis and have been determined by factors dealing with market forces. However, in 1990 a provision of the Internal Revenue Code was enacted, which provided that the valuation in a buy/sell agreement at less than fair-market value will be recognized if certain requirements are met. Another benefit to the estate under a plan of this kind is that it provides the liquidity needed to pay the obligations that arise as a result of the death of the shareholder.

With the possible severe impact of estate taxes on a family, the federal estate tax law provides certain kinds of relief for business owners. Under Section 303 of the federal tax code a company may purchase its stock from the estate of a deceased shareholder without the risk of any of the payments being considered as a dividend, for income tax purposes. However, such payments to the estate cannot exceed the aggregate of the amount of estate taxes and the funeral and administration expenses incurred by the estate. One requirement under this provision is that at least 35 percent of the adjusted gross estate must consist of the business interest in question. Under these circumstances, cash can be made available from a business to ensure the orderly liquidation of any such debts that may arise.

Under normal circumstances, estate taxes are required to be paid to the federal government within nine months after one's death. However, if the adjusted gross estate consists of a closely held business interest, and if the value of this interest exceeds 35 percent of the adjusted gross estate, the estate may qualify for a deferral of tax payments. Under such deferral, no payment of estate taxes will be due until five years after the normal due date for the taxes owed on the value of the business included in the estate. The only payments made to the federal government during this first five-year period are interest payments on the unpaid balance of the taxes due. Thereafter, the taxes related to the closely held business can be paid over ten equal annual installments. Therefore, a portion of the tax can be deferred for as long as fourteen years from the original due date. Interest, however, will be charged on the deferred payments, but presently the interest rate is only 4 percent on the tax related to the first $1 million of the closely held business interest.

It is therefore critical that the owner of a business plan ahead so that the estate is in a position to take advantage of these preferred sections of the law.

A significant method of reducing estate taxes is to place a standstill on the amount of appreciation an asset will undergo in the future. Giving away an asset of this kind is one method of stopping such impact. An interest in a business may be the most significant appreciable asset owned by an individual. However, the giving away of an asset of this kind is not simple. One must be aware of the potential traps that may exist in transfers of such interests this kind. For example, the government may dispute the valuation of the property transferred. Stringent regulations have been promulgated covering this area of the tax law. As such, these transfers should not be done without professional assistance in order to remove the possibility of having any part of such transferred asset included in the estate of the person who had previously made the gift.

CHAPTER XII

ESTATE PLANNING FOR FAMILIES WITH HANDICAPPED CHILDREN

Estate planning for the future security of a disabled child is essential, and parents of disabled children face unique planning problems in this regard. Under "normal" circumstances, parents plan for their children to become financially independent. This is not the case when a child is mentally or physically disabled. Often, a handicapped child will need various types of medical support and supervision for life. For most parents this can be difficult to deal with, both financially and psychologically. Under these circumstances the certainty that proper arrangements are in place in the event of the death of the parents is crucial, for two reasons: First, there must be adequate safeguards to protect the assets of the estate from health-care costs; second, there must be full consideration for the future welfare of the disabled child.

The problem with leaving any property outright to a disabled child is keeping it from being taken by the local, state, or federal government as reimbursement for provided services. A child that has assets or income may not be eligible for the various government entitlement programs unless the respective amounts are at the minimum threshold levels. Therefore, if a disabled child has access to financial resources these will become the primary source of support until they are spent down. Given the enormity of the costs of health-care in today's society, a handicapped child could easily exhaust an inheritance in a short period of time.

What about the impact of this situation on the brothers and sisters of a disabled child? Their inheritance might be substantially affected by the requirements and needs of a handicapped sibling. Most parents believe in equal birthrights for all their children. However, in the case of a permanently disabled child, this may not be the most sensible route to take.

In our country today there exist federal, state and local entitlement programs which provide for many necessary services for the handicapped, without cost, if the recipient does not own resources over permitted minimum levels. However, recipients who exceed the permissible minimum can qualify after their resources are used up. Therefore, it is generally not good estate planning to leave any part of an estate for the care of a disabled child if it will just be quickly consumed.

Parents are then faced with the dilemma of maintaining the child's eligibility for government entitlement programs while providing the future financial security needed. In many cases, the most sensible alternative is simply to disinherit the child and let federal, state, and local governments take over complete care. The decision to disinherit a disabled loved one, however, may be very difficult. Further, there is still no guarantee, in the case of disinheritance, that the disabled child will be treated with the level of care the parents may have wished.

There are a few alternatives that provide some security while protecting the disabled child's share of assets of the estate from health-care costs. One way to ensure the proper care of a disabled child, and protection of the estate property, is through the use of a trust. A discretionary trust keeps possession of and access to the trust property out of the child's hands, while providing a fund for the child's needs.

A discretionary trust could be established which provides the disabled child with a life estate in the trust income and principal. In a discretionary trust, the trust's assets and income are not considered the property of the beneficiary until the trustee decides so. Thus, the trust only provides funds to the disabled child at the trustee's sole and absolute discretion. This protects both the undistributed trust income and the trust property from the applicable authorities providing services, because the beneficiary is deemed to own nothing. Upon the death of the disabled child, the balance of the trust property can then be distributed to either the issue of the disabled child or, if none, to the child's siblings. Additionally, during the term of the trust, the benefits from it can be sprinkled to the siblings of the disabled beneficiary or to other family members. It is important in every discretionary trust to insert a provision which provides that if the trust's assets are attacked by creditors, the trust will terminate and the assets distributed to the remainder beneficiaries.

In the vast majority of states in this country, the assets of a trust, no matter what type of trust it may be, discretionary or otherwise, must be exhausted for the benefit of the disabled beneficiary before government funds will be made available. A minority of states, such as New York, favor the theory that government funds are entitlements, and that creators of trusts do not intend their assets to be used where public programs are available.

Another useful vehicle, which may be available in some states, is a community type trust. Which is usually established by not-for-profit organizations specifically for individuals with developmental disabilities, and provides a means by which parents of disabled children are able to pool their money on a joint basis. The attraction of this type of vehicle is that families with small estates can avoid the expense of trust creation and administration by using already established trusts. In addition, these trusts provide a conduit for parents who have no other children to act as trustees. After the termination of the trust, which usually is at the time of the death of the handicapped child, a portion of the balance remaining at such time is retained by the community trust and used for future staff and guardian costs.

It is essential in estate planning for a family that has a handicapped member, that a will must be made to ensure against the outright inheritance by such person under the laws of intestacy.

CHAPTER XIII

ELDER-CARE PLANNING

Advancements in medical science have increased our lifespan, thereby setting the stage for people to out-live their mental capacities for making financial and health-care decisions. The need for continuity in the management of one's assets is not often addressed, even though it is an important aspect of financial planning. A useful tool available to ensure proper management of one's financial affairs is a "durable power of attorney." In addition, a person can desig-nate an agent to make health-care decisions in the event of incapacitation. There are two available meth-ods of providing advance directives for health-care decisions: the "living will" and the "health-care proxy."

DURABLE POWER OF ATTORNEY

A power of attorney is a legal document that gives another person (attorney-in-fact, or, agent) broad powers over one's financial affairs whether the principal is incapacitated or not. A power of attorney can continue to be effective legally when the principal becomes disabled or incapacitated, and is therefore called "durable." The laws of most states provide that the authority of the agent will not be revoked as a result of the disability of the principal. The power may be revoked at any time by the principal, and therefore the document should be prepared with provisions specifically setting forth the principal's desires. A power of attorney can be made to become legally effective only when a designated third party has determined that a certain or "springing event" has occurred whereby the principal has become incapacitated. So, the power of the principal's property is not immediately granted. The disadvantage in this instance is what defines the "springing event." This can be complicated and time-consuming, and can thereby negate one of the important advantages of the power, which is the avoidance of judicial proceedings.

The durable power of attorney can also be used for estate-planning purposes. For example an inter vivos trust can be created with the transfer by the settlor of a minimum amount of assets. At the same time the settlor can create a power of attorney containing a provision that upon the incapacitation of the settlor, the agent shall have the right to transfer (pour-over) all other assets of the settlor into the trust, which can then continue to be administered for the benefit of the principal, family members, or other beneficiaries. Trusts of this kind are sometimes referred to as "stand-by trusts." The power to make gifts, including charitable gifts, can be provided in the durable power of attorney, as well. This feature can be very critical in one's financial plan for the purposes of maximizing the available use of the "Unified Credit" and the "Annual Exclusion", reducing an estate that may be subject to transfer taxes, creating eligibility for government benefit programs, or simply carrying out the principal's planned program for lifetime giving.

LIVING WILLS AND HEALTH-CARE PROXIES

An individual has the right to refuse medical treatment, including life-sustaining medical care. An incapacitated person's decision to refuse treatment, if the decision was made while still competent, must be honored if it can be proven by "clear and convincing evidence." A living will can provide such evidence.

The three areas that are usually of significance in determining whether an individual wishes treatment to be employed are (1) nutrition and hydration; (2) the administration of pain medication; (3) the use of other methods of prolonging life, such as machines.

The living will must be complete and specific as to the particular medical treatment one wants or does not want and should describe the circumstances under which an individual would like to have life-sustaining medical procedures terminated.

The health-care proxy laws in many states permit an adult, while competent, to delegate the right to make medical treatment decisions to another adult who will act as a surrogate decision-maker in the event of the principal's incapacity. The health-care proxy covers all decisions about health care, not just decisions about life-sustaining treatment. The health-care agent can also be given the right to make decisions concerning artificial nutrition and hydration. Usually, if the health-care agent is not aware of the principal's wishes concerning nourishment and for water provided by feeding tubes, the agent will not be able to make decisions about these measures.

A living will is a document that provides specific instructions about health-care treatment and is generally used to declare one's desire to refuse life-sustaining treatment under certain circumstances. In contrast, a health-care proxy allows one to choose someone to make those decisions on their behalf, without specifying in advance how these decisions should be made. Indeed, the health-care agent can interpret one's wishes as medical circumstances change, in order to make decisions that no one could have anticipated.

If one contemplates a health-care proxy together with a living will (which documents should be complementary and not contradictory), the living will can then serve to provide instructions and will guide the health-care agent's decisions. Health-care proxies and living wills can be changed or cancelled at any time.

MEDICAID PLANNING

At present, we have no legal statutes providing for sheltering a family from catastrophic-illness costs. These kind of expenses can arise for either home or nursing-care costs. The Medicare system does not make provisions for exposure to costs of this kind.

Currently, the only available source for funds of this kind of service is Medicaid, which is a program, jointly sponsored by the federal and state governments, created for the indigent population. Under Medicaid, eligibility requirements are met if an applicant's income and resources (assets) are below the minimum requisites. Because of these thresholds, people will alter their financial condition to achieve levels that will permit them to qualify. By transferring these resources, they are therefore made available for transfer to the heirs. There is a waiting period before the benefits will be made available after the transfer of assets, and this period can be as long as thirty months. The period of ineligibility will be measured by taking the total amount of the resources transferred by a person and reducing it by the costs that will be incurred for the care of the individual in the particular facility. All states have what is called a "deeming statute," which means that all the assets of a couple are considered to be combined. Therefore, under the Social Security Act, each spouse has financial responsibility for the other's medical-care costs. The community spouse, the one who is not institutionalized, is permitted to keep an exempt amount of assets, normally an amount determined by the state. As well, the community spouse is usually permitted an exempt monthly income.

When an individual contemplates applying for Medicaid they usually transfer their assets to their children in the form of a trust or outright gifts, in order to permit qualification. If they choose the device of a trust, the trustee cannot be given the right or the discretion to distribute any of the principal of the trust back to the settlor. Under the Social Security Act, the maximum amount which could be distributed from a discretionary trust to its settlor under the terms of the trust, (assuming full exercise of discretion by the trustees), will be considered available to the settlor for Medicaid eligibility purposes, regardless of whether (1) the discretion is actually exercised; (2) the trust is irrevocable; (3) the trust is established for purposes other than permitting the settlor to qualify for medical assistance.

Trusts created by a Medicaid applicant's spouse, which permit discretionary payments to the applicant beneficiary, will not qualify under the Act.

The transfer of assets in order to qualify for Medicaid does not preclude the fact that the gift tax may be imposed if the value of the gift exceeds the available credits allowed. Additionally, the assets transferred could become subject to any creditors of the persons receiving them.

Pursuant to the rules covering transfer of assets for Medicaid services, they can be transferred immediately before applying for non–institutional services, without a waiting period. The Medicaid period of ineligibility deals with institutional services only. The rules apply the same penalty period for institutional services for transfers of homesteads as they do for transfers of other assets. However, homesteads may be transferred to certain relatives without having a waiting period: a spouse; a child under twenty-one, or a blind or disabled child; an adult child who has resided in the home for at least two years immediately before the parent's institutionalization; or to an applicant's brother or sister, if they have an ownership interest in the homestead and have resided there for a period of one year before the applicant was institutionalized.

CHAPTER XIV

PLANNING
STRATEGIES

This section contains a discussion of certain planning strategies and devices that may be considered for estate and gift planning purposes.

GIFTS DURING LIFETIME

Annually, each individual can give up to $10,000 (the "Annual Exclusion" amount) to each of an unlimited number of persons; this amount can be doubled to $20,000 if married couples split their gifts. This method of giving is probably the simplest and the most effective planning strategy to reduce one's estate. It affords the donor the ability to choose the timing of and the amount of the gift. In addition to the permissible annual exclusion there is the lifetime exemption, or "Unified Credit" amount, of $600,000 which can be given away free of federal gift and estate tax. Three important reasons for considering lifetime gifts of the Unified Credit amount are (1) the value of the transferred property is measured at the time of the transfer, so that future appreciation in the hands of the recipient can escape transfer taxation; (2) as Congress has talked about substantially reducing the Unified Credit, it could be legislated out of existence and therefore, would not be available in the future; (3) lifetime gifts may be structured so that the federal gift tax will apply only to the net value of the gift.

IRREVOCABLE LIFE INSURANCE TRUSTS

Death in and of itself can be costly and may be a catalyst for the payment of a number of obligations. One of these is estate taxes, which can erode wealth by reason of a property owner's demise. The ownership of life insurance can protect a family's assets against such erosion. There are other reasons for acquiring life insurance, which include (1) creating an estate; (2) providing an illiquid estate with liquidity; (3) providing the ability to meet obligations under business agreements for the purchase of a deceased owner's interest; and (4) protecting a business against the loss of a key employee. The existence of the unlimited estate tax marital deduction, in addition to the Unified Credit, may lead many people to believe that the creation of an insurance fund may not be necessary. This can be a harmful misconception, however. Complete reliance on the marital deduction and Unified Credit may not prove to be in the family's best interest as a result of the dual impact of the increased longevity that may be expected of the surviving spouse and the effect of inflation. Adequate protection is even more important where there is a loss of the marital deduction through divorce or death. Since life insurance can be sheltered against death taxation, it should be considered for every estate plan.

Life insurance proceeds would be subject to estate taxation if the proceeds were payable to one's estate or if the insured person possessed or owned at the time of death any "incidents of ownership" in the insurance policy. "Incidents of ownership" usually includes the right to change the beneficiary, borrow against the surrender value of the policy, and surrender or assign the policy.

With proper planning, however, the entire proceeds of an insurance policy can be protected from estate taxation, in both the estate of the insured and that of a surviving spouse, by transferring the policy to an irrevocable life insurance trust. This results in less estate tax, more income for the survivors, and eventually, a larger amount of assets for the insured's descendants. To avoid having the proceeds of the insurance policy included in the insured's estate as a "gift in contemplation of death", the insured must survive the transfer to the trust for a period of more than three years after all incidents of ownership in the policy have been transferred. The gift in contemplation of death provision can also be avoided by the trust itself initially taking out, and thereafter owning, the policy with funds provided to the trust by its creator.

For gift tax purposes, gifts to an irrevocable life insurance trust of the amount of the annual premium payments, are usually considered as "gifts of a future interest." This is so because the beneficiary will not enjoy the use of the property until such time as the death of the insured. Therefore, such premium payments to the trust would ordinarily not qualify for the gift tax annual exclusion. In order to circumvent this problem, the beneficiaries of the trust must be given the right to demand that the trustee pay over to them their proportionate share of any property gifted to the trust. Even if the right to demand any such property is limited to a short period of time, the gift will qualify for the annual exclusion. The right to make such a demand is usually known as a "Crummey Right."

Additionally, through the proper application of the annual exclusion and the $1 million "generation-skipping transfer tax exemption" each of us possesses, a grantor may be able to avoid the generation-skipping tax in an irrevocable life insurance trust. Accordingly, the irrevocable life insurance trust remains a key tool in estate-planning strategies for individuals. It is one of the few ways to pass wealth to the next generation with no transfer tax costs. At present, Congress has shown no inclination to eliminate the benefits of an irrevocable life insurance trust.

SURVIVORSHIP LIFE INSURANCE

The so-called survivorship life insurance policy is a relatively new concept, which was developed by the life insurance industry as a direct result of the introduction of the unlimited estate tax marital deduction

into the tax law. Such an insurance policy matures on
the death of the survivor of two persons, usually two
spouses. "Second to die" life insurance policies are
premised on the likelihood that, in the case of a
married couple, the estate of the first to die will
possibly escape tax altogether as the result of the
Unified Credit, working in tandem with the unlimited
marital deduction. This ability to defer payment of the
estate tax until the death of the surviving spouse
popularized the concept of survivorship life insurance.
The premiums for this type of policy are usually lower
than other life insurance costs, because the proceeds
are not paid out until two people die. The premium
payments can be structured so that after a number of
years such payments stop, and thereafter, the policy
carries itself. The "two-life" insurance policy can be
held in an irrevocable life insurance trust.

SPLIT-DOLLAR LIFE INSURANCE

The "split-dollar plan" is a life insurance policy
ownership arrangement where two parties, typically
an employer and employee, split the premium obligations and the death benefit. For business owners or
controlling shareholders of closely held corporations,
the split-dollar life insurance fringe benefit will permit
corporate dollars to be used to provide valuable life
insurance protection. This protection can include
keeping the risk portion of the death benefit out of
the estate of the insured by the use of an irrevocable
life insurance trust. Under the split-dollar plan, the
employee, or the trust, owns the policy and assigns

certain interests in the policy to the employer as collateral for the payments made by the employer. On the death of the employee, the employer receives back the cash value of the policy or the total premiums paid, whichever is greater. The beneficiary of the policy receives the balance of the policy proceeds, i.e., the face amount less the cash value (or premiums) paid back to the employer.

TRANSFERS WITH RETAINED INTERESTS

The basic theory behind "transfers with retained interests" is that, for a period of time, the grantor retains an interest in property transferred to a trust. After the term of the interest reserved by the grantor has been completed, the gift given at the time of the establishment of the trust will be transferred to the remainder beneficiaries, with the appreciation of the property escaping gift/estate taxes. However, if the grantor should die prior to the end of the period of the retained interest, the value of the property placed in trust will be added to the grantor's estate.

Under the terms of a Grantor Annuity Income Trust (GRAT) and a Grantor Retained UniTrust (GRUT), the income rights retained will either be a fixed amount of annuity payments payable at least annually or the right to receive an annual amount equal to a fixed percentage of the fair value of the property so transferred.

If the provisions of the Internal Revenue Code are followed, it is now possible to transfer a residence at reduced transfer-tax costs. A qualified personal residence trust is defined in the regulations and must

meet the five requirements set forth. As with the
GRUT and GRAT, the transferor retains the right to
use the residence for a term of years and such property passes to the designated beneficiaries at the
expiration of the trust term.

CHAPTER XV

ESTATE PLANNING CHECKLIST

Estate planning is a continuing process. Changes in financial circumstances, marital relationships, amendments to the tax laws, where we live, the lives of our children, all dictate revisions. Following is a list of questions, the answers to which give you an idea as to what state your estate may be in.

1. Have I made an inventory of my assets?
2. Are all the locations of all of my assets known to my heirs?
3. Have I made a list of emergency instructions pertaining to keys, vaults, the name of my lawyer, anatomical gifts, and burial instructions?

4. Do I know my heirs' financial requirements.
5. Have I provided for guardians for my minor children?
6. Have I made a will?
7. When did I last update my will?
8. Are the executors and the trustees named in my will the people I want?
9. Do my will and my estate plan take advantage of the maximum estate tax benefits available to me?
10. Am I concerned about the remarriage of my spouse and therefore protection for my children?
11. Do I have a program for lifetime gifts?
12. Have I made sufficient financial provisions for all those who are dependent upon me?
13. Have I made arrangements for any business interests I own?
14. Have I provided for alternative beneficiaries if there is a common family disaster?
15. Do I want charities to receive bequests from my estate? If so, have I made such arrangements?
16. Have I made adequate arrangements for my children from a prior marriage?
17. Have I made provisions for the expenses that will come about as a result of my death?
18. Have I recently consulted a professional estate planner?
19. Have I considered an estate plan that avoids probate?
20. Is life insurance a part of my estate plan? If not, why not?

CHAPTER XVI

CONCLUSION

Many people are under a misconception that "estate planning is only for wealthy people." We tend not to realize the true value of the aggregate of all our property.

People who own real estate and life insurance and who have some form of retirement benefits should have some type of planning. No matter what the level of the estate, the Unified Credit must be effectively used.

A will or other testamentary device is the cornerstone for all estate planning. No plan can succeed without such a document. A planned estate means the orderly settlement of one's affairs on the most effective cost basis and with a maximization of the transfer of wealth.

There are traditional planning procedures being used today that can reduce an estate, as well as shelter the assets from the severe impact of estate taxation.

GLOSSARY

For an understanding of estate planning, it is essential to become familiar with some of the basic terminology.

Abatement: A priority system of reducing or eliminating bequests that an estate cannot afford to pay.

Ademption: Property left to a beneficiary in a will that is no longer in the decedent's estate upon death.

Administrator: A personal representative appointed by the court to administer the estate of an intestate.

Annual Exclusion: Under gift tax laws, each person may donate to any number of persons up to $10,000 per year.

Attested Will: A will signed by a witness.

Ascendant or Ancestor: A person related to an intestate or to a claimant to an intestate share in the ascending lineal line.

Basis: What one has invested or put into property, real or personal. For tax purposes, one subtracts the basis from the proceeds of a property sale to determine the net gain.

Beneficiary: A person or entity selected by the testator to receive a portion of the estate upon the testator's death.

Bequest: A clause in a will directing the disposition of personal property other than money.

Charitable Trust: A trust created for the benefit of a charitable organization.

Closely Held Corporation: A corporation with less than twenty-five shareholders. Usually all the issued shares are held only by those who work in the corporation.

Codicil: A testamentary instrument ancillary to a will.

Collateral: A relative who traces relationship to an intestate through a common ancestor, but who is not in his lineal line of ascent or decent.

Collateral of the Half Blood: A person related to an intestate through only one common ancestor.

Community Property: A property system premised on the belief that everything acquired during marriage belongs equally to each spouse.

Contingent Beneficiary: An alternate beneficiary selected by the testator in case the primary beneficiary dies prior to the testator.

Contingent Remainder: A remainder interest which does not become possessory until a certain specified event takes place.

Corpus: Property the settlor/transferor places in the trust. (Also known as the trust res. or trust principal.)

Descendant: A person related to an intestate or to a claimant to an intestate share in the descending lineal line.

Devise: A clause directing the disposition of real property in a will. The person named to take the real property is called the devisee.

Disinheriting: When a testator cuts someone out of their will.

Distributee or Next of Kin: That person or persons who are or who may be entitled to the property of an intestate.

Elective Share: A portion of the estate which a surviving spouse is entitled to by statute.

Escheat: A reversion of property to the state if no relatives are living to inherit.

Estate Tax: A federal or state tax placed on the fair-market value of the net asset value of a descedent's estate.

Expectant Heir: One who expects to take by inheritance.

Executor or Personal Representative: The administrator named in a will.

Executory Interests: Interests that will take place in the future.

Fair-Market Value: The average value that can be placed on an asset as determined by market forces.

Fee Simple Absolute: The complete, outright right to ownership of land, present and future.

Fee Simple Determinable: Occurs when less than the complete right to ownership is held.

Future Interest: An interest in property which is not possessory in the present but which may become possessory in the future.

Heir: A person entitled by the statute to the assets of the intestate is called an heir at law.

Heir Apparent: One who is certain to inherit unless excluded by a valid will.

Heir Presumptive: A person who will inherit if the potential intestate dies immediately, but who will be excluded if relatives closer in relationship are born.

Holographic Will: A will entirely in the handwriting of the testator.

Inheritance Tax: A tax levied on the heir of a decedent for property inherited.

Inter Vivos Trust: A trust made during one's lifetime.

Issue: Offspring; children and their children.

Kiddie Tax: The Federal Tax Code provision that any unearned income of a child is taxed at the child's parent's rate.

Lapse: An inheritance "lapses" when the intended beneficiary predeceases the testator.

Legacy: A clause in a will directing the disposition of money.

Life Estate: An estate in property which will end upon the death of a person.

Noncupative Will: An oral will.

Personal Property: Holdings such as furniture, jewelry, stock, cash and other items of personal possession.

Pick-Up Tax (Sponge Tax): Permits the state in which one dies to receive a portion of the estate taxes that would have been paid to the federal government.

Present Value: The current value of future interest or right.

Probate: The procedure by which a transaction alleged to be a will is judicially established as a testamentary disposition, and also applies to the administration process of an estate.

Prospective Heir: One who may inherit but may be excluded.

Real Property or Real Estate: Buildings and land constitute what is known as real property or real estate.

Res or Principal: The property the settlor/transferor places into a trust.

Residuary Clause: A blanket contingency clause in the will, which prevents any property from failing to be inherited.

Settlor: The person who creates a trust.

Statute of Descent and Distribution: An intestate law that applies to both real and personal property.

Succession: The process of becoming beneficially entitled to the property of a decedent.

Trust: A legal entity created to control the distribution of property.

Trustee: The person holding legal title to a trust for the benefit of a beneficiary.

Uniform Probate Code: A model statute governing the distribution of estate assets. This may be adopted, used as a guide, or wholly ignored by the various states.

Will: An expression, either written or oral, of a person's intentions concerning the disposition of property at death.

Will Substitutes: Property that will pass on death but does not pass through probate.